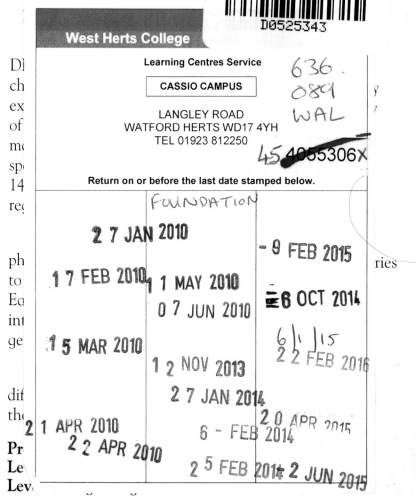

Dl
ch
ex   y
of
m(
sp(
14
re(

ph   ries
to
Ea
int
ge

dif
th(

Pr
Le
Lev

Level 3: Reading alone
Level 4: Proficient readers

The "normal" age at which a child begins to read can be anywhere from three to eight years old, so these levels are intended only as a general guideline.

No matter which level you select, you can be sure that you are helping children learn to read, then read to learn!

www.dk.com

Created by Leapfrog Press Ltd

Project Editor Naia Bray-Moffatt
Art Editor Andrew Burgess
Photography John Daniels

For Dorling Kindersley
Senior Editor Linda Esposito
Managing Art Editor Peter Bailey
US Editor Regina Kahney
Production Josie Alabaster

Reading Consultant
Cliff Moon M.Ed.

Published in Great Britain by
Dorling Kindersley Limited
80 Strand, London WC2R 0RL

8 10 9 7

Eyewitness Readers™ is a trademark of
Dorling Kindersley Limited, London.

A CIP catalogue record for this book is
available from the British Library.

ISBN-13: 978-0-7513-5899-5(pb)

Colour reproduction by Colourscan, Singapore
Printed and bound in China by L.Rex Printing Co., Ltd

The publisher would like to thank the following:
Additional design: Jane Horne
Models: Rachel Walker, Andrew Burgess, Karen Clifford,
Harry and Jack Clifford, Philippa Parsons,
Animal handler: Carolyn Fry
Additional photography by Tracy Morgan, Dave King,
Andreas Einsiedel, Bob Langrish, Ray Moller, Andy Crawford,
Steve Shott and Andrew Burgess.

 **READERS**

Animal Hospital

Written by Judith Walker-Hodge

A Dorling Kindersley Book

One day Jack and Luke
were playing near their house
when they heard a strange noise.
They went to see what it was.

"It's a duck," said Luke.

"Its wing looks hurt."

"We shouldn't move it," said Jack.

"Let's get Dad."

Dad got a cardboard box.
He put the duck gently
into the box.
Then the family drove to
the animal hospital.
"Quack! Quack!" said the duck.

WEST HERTS COLLEG
CONTROL 212100
ITEM 45 4055306x
CLASS 636.039
DATE 11·6·09
£2·99
quack quack

"Poor thing," said Mum.

"I think she's scared."

"She's just been in a car
with Dad driving!" laughed Jack.

Mallard ducks

The duck in this story
is a female mallard duck.
Male mallard ducks are more colourful.
They have green heads and yellow beaks.

"Hello," said the vet. "I'm Anna Corby. What have we got here?"
She took the duck out of the box and examined it carefully.

Bird wings

Wing bones are fragile. They are mostly hollow which means they are light. This makes it easier for birds to fly.

"She's hurt her wing," said the vet.
"But luckily it isn't broken."

The vet
strapped the wing
to the bird's body
with a bandage.
"It will take
about three weeks
to heal,"
she told the boys.

Andrew, one of the nurses,
took the duck
to a special area at the back
"All the birds are kept here,
he said.

Vet training
It takes five years to train to become a vet. Vets need to know how to care for lots of different animals.

"This is Gertie the goose. She swallowed a fish hook but she's all better now.

Has your duck got a name?"

"No," said Jack, "not yet."

"How about Jemima?" Luke suggested.

"Yes," Jack nodded.

"Maybe Gertie and Jemima can be friends!"

The nurse put some pellets and
fresh water on the ground
next to Jemima.
"Can we come and visit her?"
Luke asked.
"Sure," said the nurse.
"Come back
next week."

"Thanks!" said the boys.
They rushed inside
to tell their parents.

Jack's friend Alice was
in the waiting room.
She was holding
a rabbit.
On the floor
beside her
was a basket.

"Look what I've got!" said Alice.
Jack opened the basket and
out jumped five kittens!

"We've brought them for a check-up," said Alice's mum. "Can you help carry the kittens into the vet's room?"

"Hello again," said the vet
as the boys came in.
"They're helping Alice,"
explained Alice's mum with a smile.
The vet listened to each kitten's
heart and lungs with her stethoscope

She looked into their eyes and ears and checked their fur for fleas.

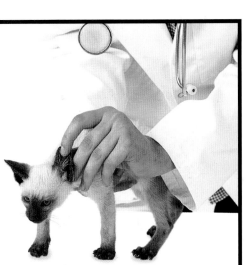

Then she gave each kitten a jab to protect it against cat flu and other illnesses.

Caring for cats

Cats need their fur checked often for fleas. They need to be checked for worms too.

Next, it was the rabbit's turn.

"He's not eating," Alice told the vet.

Anna looked inside
the rabbit's mouth.

"I think I know what the problem is,'
she said.

"His teeth are too long – no wonder
he can't chew his carrots!"
She clipped the teeth with
a pair of special scissors.
"It doesn't hurt him, I promise,"
she told the children.

Rabbit teeth

A rabbit's teeth never stop
growing. That's because
in the wild they eat
tough plant stems which
wear their teeth down.

quack
quack

The next week, Jack and Luke
went back to the hospital.
Jemima was now waddling around
the yard, quacking happily.

"She can't swim yet because of the bandage," Anna told the boys.

"Her webbed feet will crack
if they get too dry.
Would you like to help
sponge them?"
"Yes!" said the boys.
But just then a siren went off.

ring ring ring

The boys followed Anna
to the animal ambulance.
"What have we got?"
she asked the nurse.
"A dog's been hit by a car.
His front leg
looks broken."

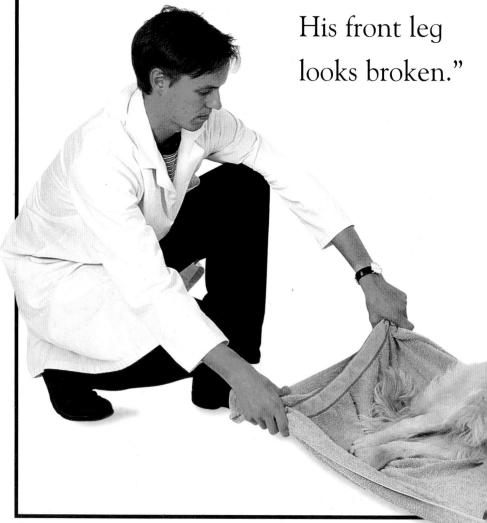

X-rays
These are special
photographs taken by
invisible rays. They
pass through the body
and show the bones.

"We'll need to
take some X-rays
right away,"
said the vet.
"Let's get him
inside."

Anna showed the boys the X-rays.
"Look," she pointed.
"Can you see the broken bone?"
Jack and Luke nodded.
"I'll have to mend it by operating.
You two wait outside."

Anna made sure everything was clean. She put on a gown and a special mask.

Then she scrubbed her hands.

"The dog will be fine," said the vet after the operation.

Two weeks later, Jack and Luke
went back to visit Jemima.
They watched the vet
take off the bandage and
check Jemima's wing.

"She's ready
to go home,"
said the vet.
"All we
have to do
is find her one."

Just then Andrew came in.
"A corn snake is missing,"
he told the vet.
"I love snakes," said Luke.
"Can I help look for it?"
"No, no," smiled Anna.
"I'm sure it will turn up."
"Does it bite?"asked Jack.
"No, corn snakes are
harmless,"
said Anna.

The next day, the vet phoned
the boys' home.
"I've found a place for Jemima
at a farm with a pond,"
she told their mother.
"Can the boys come with me?"
"Of course!" said Mum.

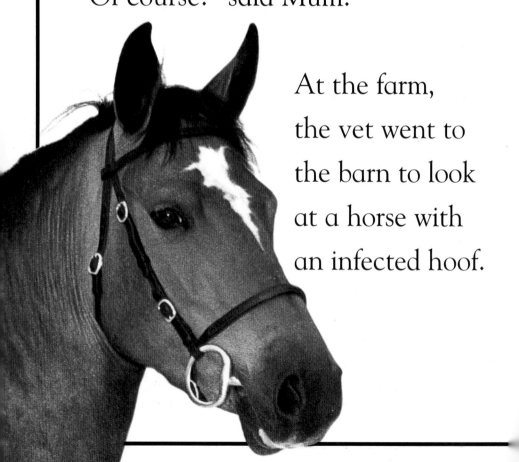

At the farm,
the vet went to
the barn to look
at a horse with
an infected hoof.

The children watched the vet
clean the horse's foot.
Then she gave the animal
a jab to fight
the infection.

"I'm almost done here,"
she said to the boys.
"Why don't you show Jemima
her new home on the pond?"

Horse shoes
Horses wear metal shoes to
stop them becoming footsore.
The job of reshoeing horses
is done by a farrier.
Shoes last 4 to 8 weeks.

Lots of ducks were swimming
in the farm pond.
Jack took Jemima out of her box.
Jemima didn't move.
"Go on, Jemima," Jack whispered.
She spread her wings,
then stepped into the pond and
swam off with her new friends.

Back at the barn,
Anna was packing her case.
"There's something moving in there!"
cried Luke.

Anna looked inside.
"You found the snake after all!"
laughed the vet.

Animal Index

Mallard ducks are wild birds that live on ponds and rivers. Some people keep ducks for their eggs. These "domestic" ducks often become pets!

Cats were first kept as pets in the Middle East about 4,000 years ago. Now there are more than 50 million pet cats in the United States alone. There are more than 100 official breeds of pet cat.

Rabbits are popular pets, and they are easy to look after. There are more than 50 breeds of rabbit to choose between.

Dogs are very loyal pets. There are more breeds of dog than any other pet animal— about 130 breeds in Britain and 160 in the United States.

Snakes make unusual pets. Corn snakes are harmless, but there are more than 400 kinds of snake that are poisonous.

Horses have been kept by people as a means of transport for over 3,000 years. Today there are more than 75 million farm horses and 100 different breeds of horse.